Praise for *Girl.*

Girl. by Anastasia DiFonzo is an incisive n
beauty, and violence that both beget. Each
sort of mirror -- a mirror that the author e
smashes, or, most intensely-places the reader
demanding they peer deeply, and discover the hidden parts of
themselves in the cracked glass.

Megan Falley, author of *Drive Here* and *Devastate Me*

In her second poetry chapbook, Anastasia DiFonzo deftly unravels and reforms our understandings of desire, shame, generational wounds, and bodily identity. Much like the actual lived experience of girlhood for so many, *Girl.* is both jagged and soft, aggrieved yet full of longing.

Sierra DeMulder, author of *Ephemera*

Anastasia DiFonzo's raw and unflinching poems are not only poems of the body, but speak to the sometimes heartbreaking resiliency it takes to inhabit a body in girlhood through womanhood. DiFonzo's collection holds a keen sense of awareness, an unwavering honesty, and a fierce attention to detail. These poems look you in the eye and do not look away.

Sheleen McElhinney, author of *Every Little Vanishing*

Girl.
© Copyright 2024 by Anastasia DiFonzo

All rights reserved. No part of this book can be reproduced in any form by any means without written permission. Please address inquiries to the publisher:

> Gnashing Teeth Publishing
> 242 E Main St
> Norman AR 71960
> http://GnashingTeethPublishing.com

Cover Artwork: Andrew Hilliard based on the artwork of Williams Worcester Churchill found at https://commons.wikimedia.org/wiki/File:Seated_Nude_by_William_Worcester_Churchill.jpg

Author Photo: Kayleigh McCollum

The cover font is: Adobe Script

The interior font is: Verdana Pro Condensed

Printed in the United States of America.

ISBN: 979-8-9875694-8-1

Non-Fiction: Poetry

A Gnashing Teeth Publishing First Edition

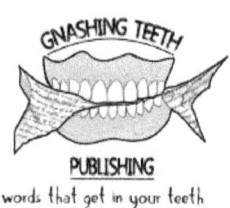

Girl.

Table of Contents

Hysteria	1
Little	2
I Asked What Is Girlhood to You	3
Girl	4
Nineteen	5
Shame as a Front-Facing Camera	6
Poem in Place of a Poem	8
We Who Once Were Thin	9
Girls in Movies Never Eat	10
Woman in Parts	12
Mannequin	14
Stripped	15
Where It Ends	17
My Abuser Teaches Me About Myself	19
Mirror	20
Not a Pretty Girl	21
Once, When I Was Pretty	22
Shame as Grandma's Lipstick	23
Self-Portrait as Bertha Mason	24
Declaration	25
The Laugh of the Medusa	26
Course Correction	27
Portrait of My Body as Earth	28
Glossary	30

Hysteria

From the moment we are born,
we know deep in our belly buttons,
those last remnants of our mothers in us,

know we must find other ways to speak.
We play with the boys. They don't know
why they hate us, only that we sound

like their mothers, which they've learned
are *shrill*, *nagging*, and *irrelevant*. We embody
this, proud, at least, to have an identity.

Little

Four years old
and Daddy tells me

not to wear those shorts

because boys
have eyes. Be careful,

you're a pretty little girl.

That night, I dream
of dancing, of hips

that don't yet exist

circling the air
as Daddy claps.

This sort of thing

is just for him.
My mother, still

saturated in the

generational
dirt that sticks

to all girls

when they're born,
agrees with him

on this alone.

I Asked What Is Girlhood to You

After Sierra DeMulder. Answers crowdsourced from the author's Instagram. Italics denote direct quotes.

Blood, pain, and commiseration.

To be *seen as lesser* than the boy who pulled my ponytail in class
    because he wanted to.
The soft bond between collateral children.

A mask I wish I could have taken off and put back on whenever I
    wanted,
or the truest and most constructed thing a person can be.

Vital to the human experience.

Divine.

Girl

I could recount every crevice
of my stepfather's cracked hands,

could place you in my childhood

bedroom and let you feel them yourself.
I could detail what it was to be fifteen

and not know better.

But you will learn. Little girl,
do not read this poem. Do not listen

to how I whispered, hand on his chest,

soft eyes meeting his, *I miss you*.
Do not picture my tattered shirt,

only pretending to cover my nipples.

Do not imagine them erect.
You will learn, soon, what it is to be a girl

in a body. For now, stand in the rain

in a white shirt with nothing to hide.
Do not think of having nothing

to hide. In time, you will eat the apple.

Let them blame you. Let them turn
from their own wretched hunger

to your undeniable innocence.

They will deny it. Soft girl,
do not let them make you hard.

Nineteen

Arms bare against
an innocent July,

I reach for a parent
to embrace and believe

I am safe.

I am nineteen
and still chase sun,

wake early to pick

the day's first flowers,
skip to work

like I once skipped

to school. Exhale
into the child

I still am. Forget

my body has grown.
Forget completely

because I am home.

Stepfather looms
in the doorway,

arms wide as an open jaw.

Shame as a Front-Facing Camera

Her lips part, corners wilted
to a pout that wants to say *I don't care,*

but everyone knows only anxious girls

play it cool. Her eyelids drop,
weighed down by a deep grey *fuck off.*

She places her index finger

at the center of her collar and yanks,
leaning forward in such a way

that her newly formed breasts

might spill out of her shirt.
She snaps the photo. I watch

as she learns what I already know:

the weight of her past rests
beneath her chin. Her jawline is buried

beneath a thousand love-me-nots.

A good girl bathed in generations
of dirty secrets held so close

they've become her. How they betray

her now. At seven, she lied
to her teacher, said she still waded

through grief's murky waters,

still woke each morning expecting
her father's fist to land on someone

(anyone), and learned of death

all over again when it didn't. The truth
is, her body ached from swallowing so much.

She wanted to go home. Wondered if

that is not enough to be excused
from this life. She gazes back into her own

shadowed eyes and cradles her breath

like a mother cradles her newborn.
What if I die, too? She asks

as if I can stop her, as if I even exist.

Poem in Place of a Poem
After Franny Choi

The edge of my desk in first grade.
The chafed crotch of my jeans.

The shape of my best friend.

A girl keeping secrets with girls,
unaware that we would be

poster children for the next

generation of Rorschach tests.
The unbridled innocence of our lives

and the embracing of all things ephemeral.

We willed ourselves to the edge of ecstasy,
and from the moment we arrived,

we were too old to stay.

We Who Once Were Thin

don't recognize the ankle
that does not fit
in the lace-up shoe.

The gaps of skin, round and
pre-lipstick pink; crevices born
from too much trying.

What secrets live there?
Once, the mountains of my body
were all clavicle and knuckle.

All women who have grown say
this, as though pronouncing it
will justify what we've become.

We who once were thin learned
to hide from eyes that all but tore off
our skin if we weren't careful.

Everyone wanted in.
Things are different now,
we are safe.

For the most part.

Girls in Movies Never Eat

The camera pans to a plate
empty as the lead girl's
stomach the first night

she learned to chuck
her dinner down the toilet.
We don't see her face,

just the rise and fall
of her hand on the fork.
It's a cinematic trick

to make you think
that you, too, can be
hospital-bed thin

and alive.
I used to see myself
in movies, the arch

of my knees
the same shape
as the girls'

on the screen,
belly tucked
into doll-sized clothes.

I, too, have shuffled
my fork, smeared
sauce on my plate

to manipulate the eye
into thinking I was full

enough to live.

The doctors didn't care
that I was dying,
only that I was

just within normal range.
Now, I am on the other
side of *just—*

like that, my legs
no longer leave
that negative space

for the perfect arch;
now, they grow,
filled with sweet butter.

I say I'm changed,
rehearse self-love
in the mirror

like the feminist
I think I am,
eat the burrito

and pretend to savor it.
But hold a knife
to my own throat

after each swallow,
curse the curves
of my belly and the soft

sag of my thighs.
Girls in movies never eat,
and neither do I.

Woman in Parts

I.

Hearing a gunshot early this morning
and thinking how you just told a man on an app

the exact corner you live on, because he asked,

and now you're weighing whether it's safer
to cancel your date because he gets mad

when girls say no, or go anyway,

because he said so, and—after all—
he does know where you live.

II.

a.
Going anyway, in part to buy yourself
time, but mostly because he called you *enchanting*,

and it's been fifty pounds since you last felt the heat

of a man's hunger. He stares at you as he eats,
and you imagine him in bed. No—

on the floor, against a wall;

anything that is hard, and you are soft,
the pillow into which he screams.

b.
Canceling because you know better,
because it's been ten years since you survived

your last death threat, and you swore you'd never

let a man hold your worth in his fist again.
You sleep at 8 pm and, in the morning,

you are alive.

Mannequin

One more squat to a perky ass
instead of this jiggling

behemoth that spilled
my boyfriend's water

the last time I tried
to turn a corner.

I love it, he says,
and I'm tempted

to fold my identity

into the excavated
blubber of my body

until I am all cleavage
and confidence.

Should he have loved
a protruding ilium

I would have stayed
empty and impenetrable

as a molded mannequin.

Stripped

At nine years old, I weighed
as much as an average

male bulldog.

I dressed in khaki pants
and an oversized jacket.

Grandma said my cheekbones

were the most beautiful
she'd ever seen,

and I cursed my flesh

for concealing them.
At twenty-six

and the size of a baby

hippo, R traced his tongue
along my shoulders,

teeth brandished

as if to tear the skin
off my collarbone.

I begged him to expose

my bones.
In this way, I was loved.

Add one more bulldog,

and you will see
what I am today. I am

everything but human.

Please, strip me
down, make me

a mole rat:

ugly and light
and held.

Where It Ends

It's eighty degrees
and I'm wearing a tank top.
The apartment's even hotter,

barely made for one body.
I see now what my mother sees:
at nineteen, I've become

a woman, grown
not from age
but from all things

that make girls
dangerous, like men
and college campuses.

I was dangerous there,
skipping through the halls,
skipping from building to building,

skipping in the quad,
skipping class to lie
in the rain with G and learn

about the body
I wanted to forget I had.
I am trying to go back;

to un-age, un-know, un-become.
To be embraced
without regard

for the thickness
of my clothing,

until my mother says,

Change, or *leave*
and don't come back.
I do not want to think

about these consequences,
so I fall into the very arms
my mother fears.

I call him *Dad*.

My Abuser Teaches Me About Myself

A found poem sourced from personal messages. Italics denote direct quotes.

You are *frustrating*. You are *afraid of other people*.
I want to unlock you, but you *are empty* and *incapable*.

You are *a master at guarding* yourself; *against what, I'm not sure*.

You are *a cosmic dance, cryptic and exclusive*.
Your mind is *a swimming pool*.

But *your soul is non-Newtonian. You are still, unnaturally*.

You *might be bad, might be pointless or shallow or empty or lame*.
But I know you are *something delicious: a beautiful girl*.

Mirror

I must believe
                      my mother broke
          the mirror
                              to protect me.
That, in the middle
             of the night,
    she kidnapped
                    it from my room
and smashed
            it into a million
                          tiny reflections
to keep me
          from becoming
                     aware, to say
that I did not need
            to see myself
                to know myself;

that, in fact,
        the fractured light
                of my body turned
     to glass could
            only cut;

even at age ten,
                    I held more depth

than   sharpness
              could   capture.

Not a Pretty Girl
Found in the song of the same name by Ani DiFranco

I am sorry
I am not dead.

Once, When I Was Pretty

Grandma said her legs would look like mine had the gravity of her life not done what gravity does, what she'd prayed it would not do to her, and I, seven, said I wished I was bigger, when what I meant was *see that I am small*, when I thought I was not small, when all I wanted was to fit inside Daddy's arms, when I knew and pretended I didn't that those arms painted the bruise on Mommy's face, when I wanted to be artwork too, when I thought to be loved was to be helpless, to need saving. When I was helpless and could not be saved. When I was fifteen and told no one the texture of my stepfather's hands. I was graceful as Grandma in her twenties, each of us floating outside our battleground bodies. We were light in this way.

Shame as Grandma's Lipstick

She was found in a pool of her own blood,
empty jug of vodka tossed, for once,
just beyond her reach, my imprint smeared

around its lip. They said it was kind
of an accident, but I know her every move
was calculated from the moment she learned

to scrape *I love you* from her own mother's
tongue. I painted her lies, desperate attempts
to be perceived as anything but herself,

made her a woman even she no longer knew.
Polished for this inevitable moment,
now she lies, forever, in a lifetime of regret.

Self-Portrait as Bertha Mason

My screams hold more weight
than the chains that bind me.

Once, you saw your future

in the depths of my eyes.
Your hunger for me was matched

only by mine for you. Captor.

You thought I would escape
my inheritance. But it came

for us both in time,

and now I am yours.
Monster. Animal. It.

Declaration

You wouldn't want me now
that I'm older and grown

to half your size. You loved me

as your lover's young daughter,
the outlawed apple you ate alone.

It would have been different

had I dined with you, growing
larger with each bite.

I've always wanted you
to be my dad. Even now,

as I write a formal list

of all the reasons to keep you
the length of the law away

from me, I just want to hug you

without considering the shape
of my nipples as they graze

your chest, or the softness

of my voice as I say,
a daughter to her dad,

I miss you. I love you.

The Laugh of the Medusa

Found in the essay of the same name by Hélène Cixous

I have been amazed since childhood,
searching with passion, each stage of rupture

something beautiful, no longer forbidden.
My desires overflow, luminous torrents

that could burst. I open my mouth, mad,
infinite, horrified, monster. I dare to speak.

I resist death. I go further. I return from afar,
from without, from below.

From childhood, body immured,
I seethe.

Course Correction

> Enter head first.
> Right onto Princess Lane.
> Stop at the tracks.
> U-turn at adolescence.
> Detour into the cloakroom. Stay hidden.
> Use the left 2 lanes to exit childhood and merge onto your new relationship with your body.
>   Warning: This road may be closed at certain times or days.
> Keep right at the fork, ignore the danger signs.
> Death Valley to the east. Headlights on. No stopping.
> Use the left 2 lanes to merge onto the future you thought you'd never see.
> Take the final exit home.

Portrait of My Body as Earth

Once, hunger's sharp knife
humbled the hills of my body,

left her smooth as Floridian earth
to be scaled by casual walkers.

She enjoyed the flow of people
ready with cameras, faces large

against her blurry backdrop.
Soon, their weight on her brittle

bones broke her, and she ached.
Famished, she formed

Alaskan mountains on her hips,
and breathless walkers

fled to flatter ground.
New life grew in their absence,

bones eclipsed by beds
of forget-me-nots, soft

as burgeoning breasts.
Though not yet welcome

in this foreign landscape,
I will not pluck her weeds,

will not carve my comfort

into her newfound curves.

I will feed her
until she is full and free.

Glossary
After Jeanann Verlee

My shame appears in disguise:
apple-red lipstick, or just an apple.

It could be the tank top I wore

the day my mother kicked me
out of her apartment for being

a slut. Here, that tank top

is freedom like boys.
Bertha Mason

is fight and captivity. She is leashed

womanhood, the swallowing
of power. Medusa is protection

and joy. Her laugh is everything

I have not known how to be:
the rupture, the torrents, the seething,

the thing I have been

taught not to say.
The little death of a girl.

Acknowledgements

Thank you to the editors of Gnashing Teeth Publishing, in which versions of the following poems originally appeared by the same or different titles:

Once, When I Was Pretty

Declaration

About the Author

Anastasia DiFonzo is an Oakland-based poet. She is a three-time Best of the Net nominee, and her debut chapbook, *A Certain Serenity*, was published by Puna Press in April of 2022. When she's not writing, she can be found having coffee with her cats.